OUT OF → THIS WORLD

VIRGINIA LOH-HAGAN

DARK

MATTER

45TH PARALLEL PRESS

Published in the United States of America
by Cherry Lake Publishing
Ann Arbor, Michigan
www.cherrylakepublishing.com

Reading Adviser: Marla Conn, MS, Ed.,
  Literacy specialist, Read-Ability, Inc.
Book Designer: Jessica Rogner

Photo Credits: © Color4260/Shutterstock, cover, 1; © NASA/NASA ID:
  PIA12348, 5; © NASA/NASA ID: PIA21073, 7; © NASA/Kimiya Yui/NASA ID:
  iss045e082789, 8; © NASA Goddard/NASA ID: GSFC_20171208_Archive_
  e001359, 11; © NASA Goddard/NASA ID: PIA07907, 12; © NASA/Kim
  Shiflett/NASA ID: KSC-20160906-PH_KLS02_0053, 15; © NASA/NASA ID:
  0302063, 16; © NASA Goddard/NASA ID: GSFC_20171208_Archive_e001033,
  19; © NASA Goddard/NASA ID: GSFC_20171208_Archive_e002070, 21;
  © MarcelClemens/Shutterstock, 23; © NASA, ESA, CXC, SAO, the Hubble
  Heritage Team (STScI/AURA), and J. Hughes (Rutgers University)/NASA
  ID: GSFC_20171208_Archive_e001791, 25; © Don Brinn/AP/Shutterstock, 27;
  © Jeremy Keith/Flickr, 29
Graphic Element Credits: © Trigubova Irina/Shutterstock

45th Parallel Press is an imprint of
Cherry Lake Publishing Group

Library of Congress Cataloging-in-Publication Data
Names: Loh-Hagan, Virginia, author. | Loh-Hagan, Virginia.
  Out of this world.
Title: Dark matter / by Virginia Loh-Hagan.
Description: Ann Arbor, Michigan : Cherry Lake Publishing, 2020 |
  Series: Out of this world | Includes bibliographical references
  and index.
Identifiers: LCCN 2020006889 (print) | LCCN 2020006890 (ebook) |
  ISBN 9781534169227 (hardcover) | ISBN 9781534170902 (paperback) |
  ISBN 9781534172746 (pdf) | ISBN 9781534174580 (ebook)
Subjects: LCSH: Dark matter (Astronomy)—Juvenile literature.
Classification: LCC QB791.3 .L65 2020 (print) | LCC QB791.3 (ebook) |
  DDC 523.1/126—dc23
LC record available at https://lccn.loc.gov/2020006889
LC ebook record available at https://lccn.loc.gov/2020006890

Printed in the United States of America | Corporate Graphics

TABLE OF CONTENTS

WHAT IS THE UNIVERSE?

The universe is huge. It's everything that exists. This includes planets, stars, and outer space. It includes living things on Earth.

The universe contains billions of galaxies. Galaxies are huge space collections. Galaxies are made up of billions of stars, gas, and dust. Galaxies include **solar** systems. Solar means sun. Earth is in the Milky Way galaxy. Galaxies spin in space. They spin very fast. There's a lot of space between stars and galaxies. This space is filled with dust, light, heat, and rays.

Before the birth of the universe, there was no time, space, or matter. Anything that takes up space is matter. Matter can exist in different states. The common states include solid, liquid, and gas. This is why things like air and smoke are considered matter. But the heat and light from a fire aren't matter. These don't take up space.

The universe hasn't always been the same size. It also hasn't always existed. Some scientists believe it began with a "big bang."

 Studying the Milky Way helps scientists understand other galaxies.

This is a **theory**. Theory means an idea. This theory explains how the universe was born. First, the universe was a super tiny blob, smaller than a pinhead! Then, that super tiny blob exploded. This happened 13.8 billion years ago. Next, energy spread out. Energy is made from matter. For example, the flames in a fire are matter. They take up space. But the heat you feel and the light you see from the flames are energy. Last, stars and planets formed. This all happened in less than a second.

Scientists think the universe is still expanding. Expanding means growing or spreading out. Scientists also think this expanding process is speeding up.

CHAPTER → ONE

WHAT IS DARK MATTER?

Stars and planets are glowing objects. They **emit** light. Emit means to give off. Glowing objects make up a small part of the universe. The rest of the matter is dark. It's hidden from people's sight. This is called dark matter. Dark matter is the stuff in the universe we can't see. It's the stuff in space that has **gravity**. Gravity is the natural force that causes things to fall toward Earth.

 The visible universe is made of protons, neutrons, and electrons that are bundled together into atoms.

Dark matter makes up about 27 percent of the universe's **mass**. Mass is the amount of material that makes up an object. The other 15 percent is made of **atoms**. Atoms are basic units of matter.

Dark matter doesn't emit or **reflect** light. Reflect means to bounce back. This makes dark matter **invisible**. It can't be seen.

There's a lot about dark matter we don't know. But there's a lot we do know. **Astrophysicists** are special scientists. They study dark matter. Astrophysics is a space science. It uses the laws of physics and chemistry. It studies the birth, life, and death of objects in the universe. It seeks to understand how the universe works.

Astrophysicists know dark matter exists because they study its pull. They study its effect on nearby objects.

 Dark matter is often used to explain what we don't know yet about space.

AMONG THE STARS: WOMEN IN SCIENCE

Dr. Regina Caputo is an astrophysicist. She works at NASA's Goddard Space Flight Center. NASA is the National Aeronautics and Space Administration. Aeronautics is the science of aircraft. She's a NASA research scientist. She was born and raised in Colorado. She graduated from the Colorado School of Mines. She earned a degree in engineering physics. She also has a doctorate in physics from Stony Brook University. She's inspired by Dr. Vera Rubin. Dr. Caputo studies gamma ray astrophysics. She finds signs of dark matter in the hearts of galaxies. She said, "I'm interested in dark matter searches, searches for new physics, and all the astrophysics one must understand before discovering something new." She also said, "We don't know [what dark matter is]. We know what it isn't. It's not made of 'normal' matter. We know it's stable. We know it's not charged. We have a range of masses that it can be. But beyond that, we haven't figured it out yet."

CHAPTER TWO

WHAT DOES DARK MATTER DO?

Scientists are learning more about dark matter. They know that dark matter acts differently than all other things. They describe dark matter as "cosmic glue." Cosmic refers to the universe.

Dark matter seems to act like a glue. It holds things together in outer space. Galaxies spin and expand. Without dark matter, galaxies could fly away. Dark matter pushes out a gravitational force on the matter around it.

Gravitational force is a push and pull. It's the thing that attracts 2 objects with mass. Every object is pulling on every other object in the universe.

 Dark matter's gravity forces gas and dust to collect. Gas and dust build up into stars and galaxies.

This pulling is the main proof that dark matter exists. The fact that galaxies don't spin out of control is proof of dark matter. Scientists know something is pushing and pulling on galaxies. They know stars and planets don't have enough gravitational force to hold the universe together. So, they believe it must be dark matter.

Scientists think dark matter explains how space objects move. Dark matter helps galaxies **rotate**. Rotate means to spin. Dark matter helps to form galaxies. Galaxies are different shapes and sizes. Dark matter controls how galaxies interact with each other.

 The Milky Way is part of the Local Group. This group of galaxies has over 30 galaxies in it.

IT'S (ALMOST) ROCKET SCIENCE

The Fermi Gamma-ray Space Telescope is a NASA spacecraft. Spacecraft is a machine in space. The *Fermi* telescope is special. It studies the most powerful sources of radiation in the universe. Radiation is energy. It's in the form of light. It's also in the form of moving particles that are smaller than atoms. The most extreme type of radiation is gamma rays. Gamma rays have the most energy. They have over 1 billion times the energy of visible light. As such, they pass right through regular telescopes. Telescopes are tools used to see objects that are far away. Gamma rays come from the most extreme places in the universe. They come from black holes. They come from exploding stars. They come from galaxy clusters. The *Fermi* telescope has two main tools. It has a large telescope that finds gamma rays. It also has detectors that observe gamma-ray bursts. Gamma-ray bursts are brief flashes of gamma rays.

CHAPTER THREE

WHAT IS GRAVITATIONAL LENSING?

The spinning of galaxies is one proof of dark matter. Another proof is **gravitational lensing**. This refers to the bending and focusing of light.

Dark matter is thought to exist in the space between the stars. Its gravitational pull influences the path of starlight traveling to Earth. Dark matter acts like a magnifying glass. A magnifying glass is a tool that zooms in on small objects to make them seem bigger.

 Scientists also study the areas around galaxies.

Dark matter bends and distorts the light from galaxies. It alters how we see things in space. It's like how water distorts the way things inside a bottle look.

Light travels from galaxies. It passes through dark matter. Dark matter is full of gravity. This gravity pulls at the light. This creates an effect called gravitational lensing. This is how scientists can "see" dark matter. They see pictures of strange rings. They see arcs of light. Normal matter does not explain the amount of distortion scientists see. Thus, this must be dark matter.

The Hubble Space Telescope is in space. It's one of the largest telescopes. Hubble has very sharp vision. It estimated how much dark matter there was in a specific galaxy cluster using gravitational lensing.

 The Hubble Space Telescope looked at a small patch of space for 12 days. It found over 10,000 galaxies.

DOWN-TO-EARTH EXPERIMENT

Want to learn more about gravitational lensing? Try out this experiment!

Learn how scientists study invisible things. Think like a space scientist!

Materials:

- 2 clear water bottles with lids
- Coins
- Water

Instructions:

1. Put several coins in each bottle.
2. Fill one jar all the way to the top with water. You don't want any air in the jar. Close the lid.
3. Place both bottles side by side. How do you know which bottle has water in it?
4. Turn both bottles upside down. The coins in the bottle with water move slower. They move differently than in the bottle without water. Notice how the bottle with water bends light. It distorts how the coins look. This is like gravitational lensing.

Think about this: The water is there. But it's invisible. It can't be directly seen. It's clear. You determine the water exists because that bottle is heavier than the other bottle. The objects in the bottle with water act differently than the objects in the bottle without water. This is how scientists study invisible things.

CHAPTER FOUR

HOW ARE HOT GAS AND DARK MATTER LINKED?

Another proof of dark matter can be found in galaxy clusters. Galaxy clusters are groups of galaxies. They're bound together by gravity. They have from 100 to 1,000 galaxies. They have hot gas. They have a lot of dark matter.

Hot gas is held in the cluster by gravity. A lot of gravity is needed to do this. Something has to be strong enough to balance the gas pressures. This gas is super hot. Temperatures are over 10 million degrees Fahrenheit (5 million degrees Celsius). The mass of the

 Superclusters are groups of galaxy clusters.

galaxies is not enough. There has to be something else. Dark matter is the something else. It provides the additional gravity.

NASA is in charge of the U.S. space program. They have a special machine. It's called Chandra. It's in space. It's the world's most powerful x-ray telescope. X-rays are waves with high energy. Chandra can detect x-rays. When matter heats up, it emits x-rays. In space, x-rays are made when matter is heated to millions of degrees.

Chandra took pictures of galaxy clusters crashing. This created lots of x-rays. Scientists studied the location of x-rays from hot gases. This way, they were able to study dark matter. They found that galaxies have a lot of dark matter packed into their cores.

The intracluster medium is the hot gas in the middle of galaxy clusters.

21

CHAPTER → FIVE

WHAT IS DARK ENERGY?

Sometimes, dark matter is confused with dark energy. But dark matter and dark energy are not the same things. Dark matter attracts gravity. Dark energy **repels** gravity. Repel means to push away.

Ever since the big bang, galaxies have kept spinning and expanding. This means other solar systems are moving away from ours. Farther systems move at greater speeds. They move in all directions. They're being pushed out by a force. If the universe was only made of galaxies, then it shouldn't be expanding.

Gravity should slow down the expanding. But it doesn't.

This means there's something out there.

 Eventually, galaxies will move too far for us to see.

There has to be some energy that makes galaxies expand. This energy has to be strong enough to overcome gravity. It's fighting gravity's pull. It's causing galaxies to speed apart from one another. Scientists call this dark energy. Dark energy explains why the universe expands. Dark matter explains how groups of objects work together.

Dark energy grows stronger as the universe expands. It's even more mysterious than dark matter. It's yet to be fully explained.

Dark energy and dark matter make up about 95 percent of the universe. The remaining 5 percent is ordinary matter. We can't see dark energy or dark matter. But scientists believe they exist.

Dark energy is a property of space. Albert Einstein was one of the first to understand that space is not empty.

25

CHAPTER SIX

WHO FIRST STUDIED DARK MATTER?

Dr. Jan Oort was a Dutch **astronomer**. Astronomers are scientists who study outer space. Oort lived from 1900 to 1992. He studied the Milky Way. He was among the first to say dark matter existed. He did this in 1932. He found that the matter seen in galaxies is less than the size of the galaxies.

A year later in 1933, Dr. Fritz Zwicky continued Oort's theory. He was a Swiss astronomer. He lived from 1898 to 1974. He studied galaxy clusters.

 Dr. Zwicky worked at the California Institute of Technology.

Dr. Zwicky said the mass of known matter in galaxies is not great enough to make the gravitational force to hold a galaxy cluster together. He said a huge mass must be holding everything together. This mass is dark matter.

No one paid attention to dark matter after that for almost 40 years. Then, Dr. Vera Rubin came along. Rubin was an American astronomer. She lived from 1928 to 2016. She studied galaxy rotation rates.

Rubin proved that galaxies are mostly made of dark matter. In 1968, she was in an **observatory** in Arizona. Observatories are places with telescopes. She was looking at the galaxy closest to ours. She noticed that stars at the outer edges were moving as fast as those in the center. She also noticed the outer stars were moving really fast. These stars should have flown apart. But something was holding them together. Rubin confirmed that dark matter had to exist. She made dark matter relevant.

 Dr. Rubin became an astronomer because she wanted to learn how the universe worked.

29

GLOSSARY

ASTRONOMER (uh-STRAH-nuh-mur) scientist who studies outer space

ASTROPHYSICISTS (as-troh-FIZ-uh-sists) special scientists who study space science that applies physics and chemistry in order to learn how the universe works

ATOMS (AT-uhmz) basic units of matter

EMIT (ih-MIT) to give off

GRAVITATIONAL LENSING (grav-ih-TAY-shuh-nuhl LENZ-ing) the bending and focusing of light that happens as it travels through dark matter toward the observer

GRAVITY (GRAV-ih-tee) force that attracts things to fall toward Earth's center

INVISIBLE (in-VIZ-uh-buhl) not able to be seen

MASS (MAS) the amount of material in an object

OBSERVATORY (uhb-ZUR-vuh-tor-ee) a building with telescopes and other equipment for the study of space

REFLECT (rih-FLEKT) to bounce back

REPELS (rih-PELZ) pushes away

ROTATE (ROH-tate) to spin

SOLAR (SOH-lur) relating to the sun

THEORY (THEER-ee) an idea meant to explain something

FAR-OUT FACTS

- Dark matter in outer space is being studied underground. The Laboratori Nazionali del Gran Sasso is in Italy. It's under Gran Sasso mountain. It's over 4,500 feet (1,372 meters) underground. It's the world's largest underground research center. It's shielded from the noise of cosmic rays that hit Earth.

- Dark matter doesn't interact. It doesn't crowd together. It doesn't form into dense objects like planets. But it does have halos. There's more dark matter in the centers of galaxies. Dark matter doesn't rotate with other space objects. So, our solar system is always moving into a "wind" of dark matter bits.

- Not much is known about dark matter. Scientists still have much to learn. As such, some people don't believe in dark matter. They call it the "stuff of science fiction." Dark matter has been featured in many video games. It's often used as material to make weapons. It's portrayed as a dark, evil force.

LEARN MORE

Tyson, Neil deGrasse. *StarTalk: Everything You Ever Need to Know About Space Travel, Sci-Fi, the Human Race, the Universe, and Beyond.* Washington, DC: National Geographic, 2017.

Tyson, Neil deGrasse, with Gregory Mone. *Astrophysics for Young People in a Hurry.* New York, NY: Norton Young Readers, 2019.

INDEX

ABOUT THE AUTHOR

Dr. Virginia Loh-Hagan is an author, university professor, and former classroom teacher. One of her favorite shows is "*The Big Bang Theory*." She lives in San Diego with her very tall husband and very naughty dogs. To learn more about her, visit: www.virginialoh.com